Australian Paramedics

Aaron White

www.childrensbooksbyaaronwhite.com
www.facebook.com/childrensbooksbyaaronwhite

DEDICATION

I dedicate this book to my beautiful wife, Francesca, and to my wonderful sons, Tyler and Jayden. I also dedicate it to all of the fantastic paramedics. You men and women do such an amazing job, and I hope this book will help to show people what you do. Thank you.

Copyright © 2019 Aaron White
All rights reserved.

ISBN-13: 978-0-994391599

Come, meet some Australian paramedics and learn about what they do.

Hi, I'm Chloe, and this is Oliver; we are paramedics. We help people, who are sick or have been injured.

This is our ambulance. We use it to transport an injured or sick person to hospital.

When we arrive at the hospital, we hand over the patient to the doctors and nurses, who will continue to help them.

Sometimes we are at events. If you hurt yourself, you can come to us for help.

If a person is injured or sick, in a remote location, the airplane can fly into the area to help them.

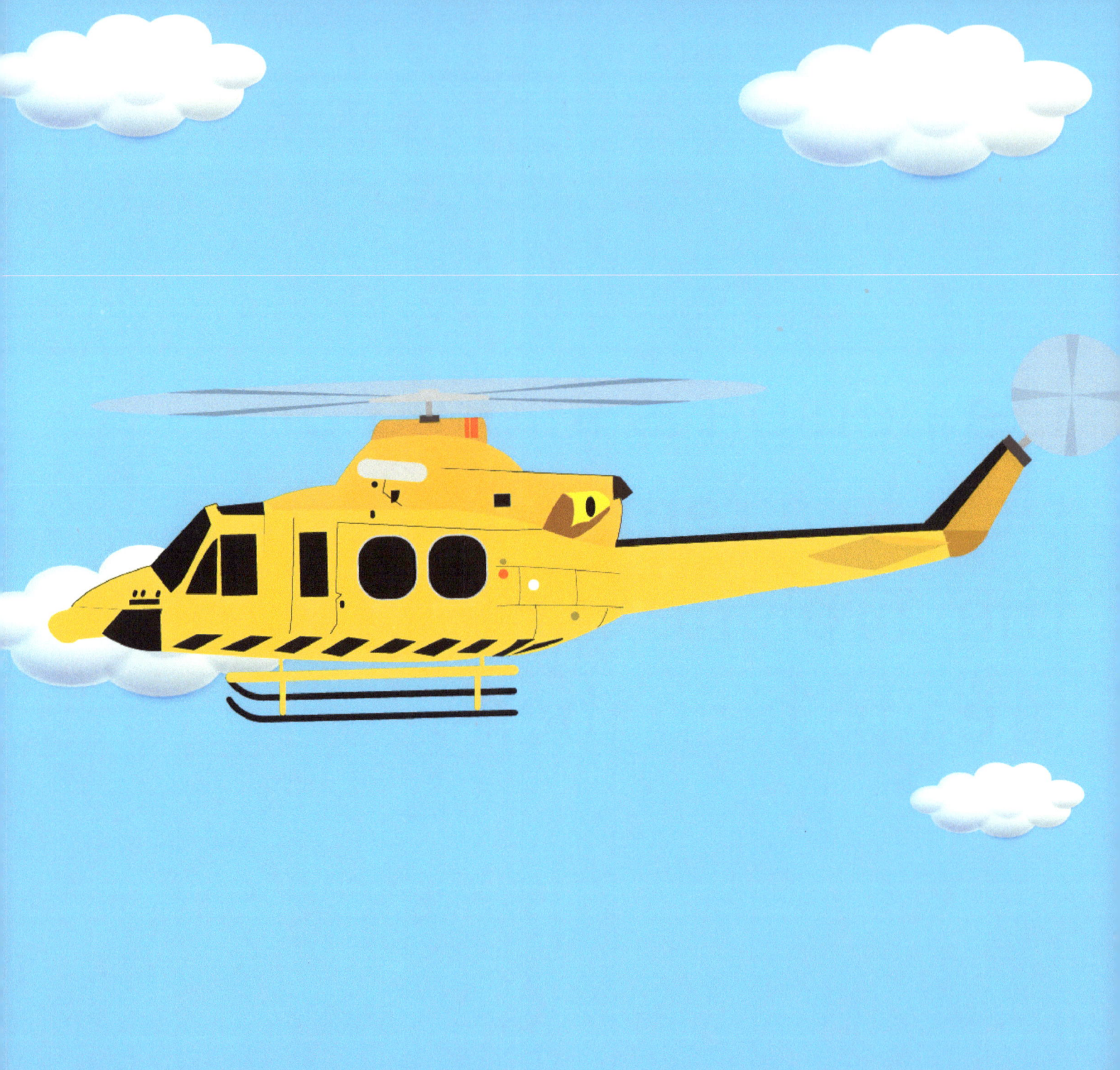

In an emergency, the helicopter can be used to fly the injured or sick person straight to hospital.

If you want to learn how to help someone, who is sick or has been injured, you can do a first aid course.

I hope that you enjoyed learning about some of the cool things we do. Maybe when you grow up, you can become a paramedic.

If there is an emergency and you need an ambulance, call 000. Here are some blank pages for you to draw some paramedics on.

www.ingramcontent.com/pod-product-compliance
Lightning Source LLC
Chambersburg PA
CBHW041439010526
44118CB00002B/126